Earth's Changing Climate

Weather and Climate Change

WORLD
BOOK

World Book
a Scott Fetzer company
Chicago

For information about other World Book publications, visit our website at www.worldbook.com or call 1-800-WORLDBK (967-5325).

For information about sales to schools and libraries, call 1-800-975-3250 (United States) or 1-800-837-5365 (Canada).

World Book, Inc.
180 North LaSalle Street
Suite 900
Chicago, Illinois 60601
USA

Library of Congress Cataloging-in-Publication Data
Weather and climate change.
     pages cm. -- (Earth's changing climate)
   Includes index.
   Summary: "Explains the science behind climate change and the effect climate change is having and may have on weather, includes glossary, additional resources, and index."-- Provided by publisher.
     ISBN 978-0-7166-2707-4
     1. Weather--Effect of human beings on--Juvenile literature. 2. Long-range weather forecasting--Juvenile literature. 3. Global warming--Juvenile literature. 4. Nature--Effect of human beings on--Juvenile literature. I. World Book, Inc.
   QC903.15.W43 2016
   551.6--dc23
                              2015028044

Earth's Changing Climate
ISBN: 978-0-7166-2705-0 (set, hc.)
Also available as:
ISBN: 978-0-7166-2717-3 (e-book, ePUB3)

Printed in China by Toppan Leefung Printing Ltd., Guangdong Province
2nd printing August 2016

Staff

Writer: David Dreier

Executive Committee

President
Jim O'Rourke

Vice President and
Editor in Chief
Paul A. Kobasa

Vice President, Finance
Donald D. Keller

Vice President, Marketing
Jean Lin

Director, Human Resources
Bev Ecker

Editorial

Director of Digital Product
Content Development
Emily Kline

Manager, Science
Jeff De La Rosa

Editors, Science
Will Adams
Echo Gonzalez

Administrative Assistant
Annuals/Series Nonfiction
Ethel Matthews

Manager, Contracts & Compliance
(Rights & Permissions)
Loranne K. Shields

Manager, Indexing Services
David Pofelski

Digital

Director of Digital Product
Development
Erika Meller

Digital Product Manager
Lyndsie Manusos

Digital Product Coordinator
Matthew Werner

Manufacturing/ Production

Manufacturing Manager
Sandra Johnson

Production/Technology Manager
Anne Fritzinger

Proofreader
Nathalie Strassheim

Graphics and Design

Senior Art Director
Tom Evans

Senior Designers
Matt Carrington
Isaiah Sheppard
Don Di Sante

Senior Cartographer
John M. Rejba

Acknowledgments

Alamy Images: 23 (eye35). AP Photo: 43 (Rob Griffith). Bridgeman Images: 19 (*The Frost Fair*, c. 1685, oil on canvas, English School; Yale Center for British Art). The Buffalo News: 11 (Derek Gee). Ittiz: 17. NASA: 15 (ISS Crew Earth Observations experiment/Image Science & Analysis Laboratory, Johnson Space Center), 21 (Jeffrey Kargel, USGS/JPL/ AGU), 25 (Pat Izzo), 39 (Jeff Schmaltz, MODIS Rapid Response Team/GSFC). NOAA: 9 (Michael Boice, OAR/ARL/ATDD). SeaPics: 27 (Gary Bell). Shutterstock: 5 (Megastocker), 7 (Matt Tilghman), 13 (Minerva Studio), 31 (smuay), 33 (Steven Van Verre), 45 (Michael Ledray). Storm and Sky: 35, 37 (Mike Hollingshead). U.S. Geological Survey: 29 top (M. T. Millet, Glacier Bay National Park and Preserve Archive), 29 bottom (R. D. Karpilo, National Park Service). White House: 41 (Pete Souza).

Table of contents

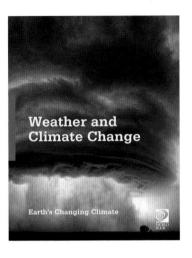

Heavy rains fall from a swirling thunderstorm in Montana.

© Sean R. Heavey

Glossary There is a glossary of terms on page 46. Terms defined in the glossary are in type **that looks like this** on their first appearance on any spread (two facing pages).

Introduction

Our daily lives are greatly affected by the weather. Sunny days, windy days, snow, rain, heat, cold. The weather changes from season to season and often from day to day. We take the weather for granted and expect those changes. It is all part of life on Earth.

But important changes are happening on our planet. Scientists have found that the world's **climate** is growing warmer. And the rising temperatures are changing the weather in many places. Some areas are getting hotter. In other places, storms are getting stronger. Deserts are growing larger. **Glaciers** are melting.

What is causing the Earth's climate to get warmer? Study by scientists suggests the warming is being caused by the release of **greenhouse gases** into the **atmosphere.** Such gases naturally trap heat near Earth's surface. Large amounts of these gases are released by things humans do, particularly the burning of **fossil fuels,** such as coal, oil, and natural gas.

This book explains the effect global warming might have on weather and climate.

Global warming vs. climate change

The words *global warming* and *climate change* are often used to mean the same thing. These words are used to mean two very closely linked ideas. Global warming is the recent, *observed* (noticed) increase in **average global surface temperatures** on Earth. Climate change means the changes in climate linked to changes in average global temperature. Global average temperature has a complicated effect on climate. Global warming will not cause every place to get warmer. Instead, it will have a variety of effects on temperature, rain and snow, and other parts of climate. These effects are together called *climate change*.

The difference between weather and climate

There is a saying that **climate** is what you expect, while weather is what you get. Over a long period, climate is fairly *predictable*. That is, we can have a good guess at what it will be like. Climate is an average of the weather conditions experienced in an area over time. Weather is the state of the **atmosphere** at a particular place and time. It can change from one day—or one hour—to the next. Weather can be a thunderstorm, a heat wave, a blizzard, or many other brief conditions.

An area's climate can usually be described in a few words. For example, Arizona is a state in the southwestern United States. Its climate is hot and dry. Florida is a state forming the tip of the southeastern U.S. Its climate is warm. Those are the typical conditions these areas experience for most of the year. Their climates and others around the world are called *regional climates.*

We can also talk about the climate of the entire Earth—the global climate. This is what global warming is all about. Climates normally take a long time to change. The global climate, however, is getting warmer from one decade to the next.

The climate in a cloud forest in Costa Rica—a country in Central America—is warm and moist.

2014: A year of record warmth

The year 2014 was the warmest year since people began keeping records in 1880. And 2014 was not unusual. The 10 warmest years on record had occurred since 1997. And nine of those years had occurred since 2000.

How warm was it in 2014? The **average global temperature**—land and sea—was 57 °F (13.9 °C). That mark was 1.24 °F (0.69 °C) above the average for the 1900's. The land temperature was the fourth highest for that time.

But the ocean temperature was at an all-time high. The average seawater temperature was 60.9 °F (16.1 °C), which was 1.03 °F (0.57 °C) above average. It was mostly the ocean temperature that caused the record warmth in 2014.

Temperatures on both the land and sea are rising.

The U.S. National Oceanic and Atmospheric Administration (NOAA) has more than 100 weather stations around the nation. Here, a station in Moose, Wyoming, in the western United States, is shown.

How do we know?

How do scientists know the yearly temperatures of the air and oceans? And especially, how do they know what those temperatures were decades ago?

The answer lies in careful record-keeping. Weather scientists have been recording temperature readings in a careful way since 1880. These *data* (facts) show a steadily warming world.

The Buffalo snowstorm of 2014

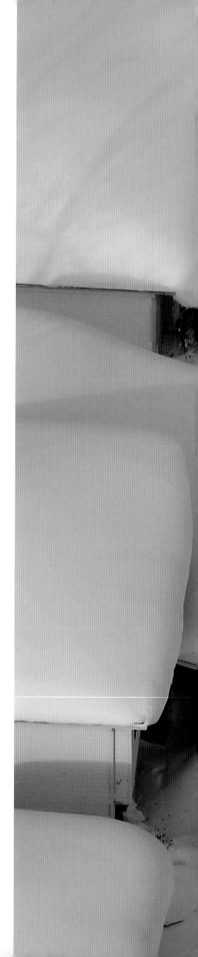

Some weather events cause many people to question whether the planet is really becoming warmer. One such event was a snowstorm in November 2014. It struck upstate New York, in the northeastern United States. The city of Buffalo and nearby towns in that area were buried in up to 7 feet (2.1 meters) of snow.

The people of Buffalo are used to heavy snowfalls. But few snowstorms in memory equaled this one. Buffalo normally gets about 8 feet (2.4 meters) of snow during an entire winter.

The snow from the storm—actually two closely spaced storms—was "**lake-effect** snow." This kind of snow happens in areas along the Great Lakes of the United States and Canada. Cold, dry winds from the north blow southward across the lakes. The air picks up moisture from the warmer water. This produces huge clouds. Over the land, the clouds release their moisture as snow. In Buffalo, air from the Arctic flowed over Lake Erie and gathered moisture.

Huge snowdrifts trapped the people of Buffalo in their homes for days. At least 13 people died from the cold or from heart attacks suffered while shoveling snow.

How can big snowstorms happen in a warming world?

The huge Buffalo snowstorm happened during the warmest year on record. How can major cold-weather events happen if the world is warming?

There is a big difference between local weather and world **climate.** A snowstorm is a weather event in one area. Global warming is a climate event occurring everywhere. It is an *average increase* in the world's temperature. Low temperatures in one area are offset by higher temperatures elsewhere. Thus, terrible cold and snow in one corner of the world does not mean that the planet is not getting warmer.

But there is more to the story than that. Although the Buffalo event was **lake-effect** snow, severe winter storms can also result from global warming. That is because global warming puts more heat into the **atmosphere.** The added heat causes increased *evaporation* (liquid water changing to water vapor, or gas) from the oceans, creating larger clouds. That can lead to strong storms, including winter storms.

A photo of a huge thunderstorm in the central United States. With climate change, extreme storms may become more common.

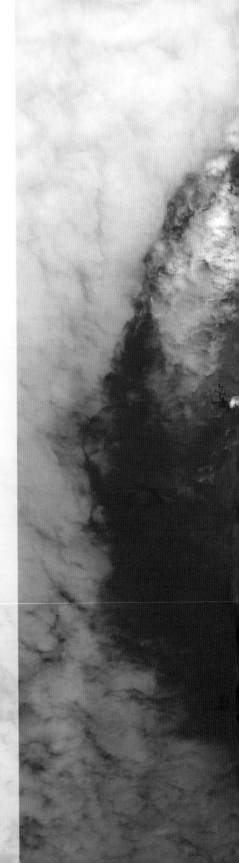

Causes of natural climate change

It may be difficult to imagine that something as big as Earth's **climate** can change. But the climate has changed many

times throughout the planet's history. There have been long periods of widespread warmth. In other times, ice has covered much of the globe.

What caused these changes? The shifting positions of the continents has been one reason. The Earth's *crust* (outer layer) is made up of **tectonic plates** that move over time. The continents that lie on these plates have been in very different positions in the past than they are now.

Changes to Earth's orbit around the sun is another reason for climate change. Volcanoes *eject* (shoot out) huge amounts of ash into the **atmosphere.** This ash can cause changes to climate for short periods. Changing levels of **greenhouse gases** have also played a role in past change.

This section of the book will examine two major events in Earth's past.

An eruption of the Sarychev Volcano in the Kuril Islands (northeast of Japan). The eruption was captured in a 2009 photograph by an astronaut on the International Space Station.

The last ice age

At least five major ice ages have occurred in Earth's history. During an ice age, temperatures fall and **glaciers** and icecaps spread. The first ice age occurred more than two billion years ago. Each ice age has lasted millions of years.

An ice age is broken up into periods that have different weather. In some periods, the **climate** is cold and ice advances. These times are called *glacial cycles.* In other periods, known as *interglacial cycles,* the climate warms, ice melts, and glaciers retreat, or fall back.

What we call the last ice age was actually a glacial cycle lasting about 110,000 years. It was part of an ice age that started about 2.4 million years ago. Many scientists think that ice age is still going on. We are in an interglacial cycle that began about 11,500 years ago.

Ice ages have had several likely causes, including the slow movement of the continents caused by **plate tectonics.** Scientists think the present ice age has been caused mostly by changes in the amount of sunlight striking Earth. These changes were caused, at least in part, from slow changes in Earth's orbit around the sun.

An illustration of what Earth may have looked like at the end of the last ice age.

How do we know?

Scientists learn about climates from times long ago in the past using different kinds of evidence. Sea-floor minerals that are the remains of tiny ocean animals provide one clue. They tell scientists which *isotopes* (types) of oxygen the animals used to make their shells. One oxygen isotope was more common in warm periods, another isotope in cold eras. Other evidence comes from ancient **pollen grains,** which show which kinds of plants lived in earlier eras. These are just two of the ways that scientists learn about past climates.

The Little Ice Age

In the 1300's, much of the world began to experience colder-than-normal winters. After a brief warming in the 1500's, temperatures fell again. The unusual cold lasted until the mid-1800's. This entire period is called the *Little Ice Age.*

During the Little Ice Age, **glaciers** grew larger in North America and Europe. Parts of Earth south of the *equator* (the imaginary line that lies between the north and south poles and that circles Earth) also experienced colder winters. The Little Ice Age caused great hardship, especially in Europe. During the 1600's, European farmers struggled to grow enough food to feed the people.

Scientists are not sure what caused the Little Ice Age. They think one cause may have been major volcanic eruptions in the **tropics.** The tropics are areas of Earth near the equator. The volcanoes threw huge amounts of ash into the air, blocking sunlight.

Frost fairs on the Thames

Life was not completely terrible during the Little Ice Age. In at least one place—London—people learned to celebrate the cold.

From the 1600's to the 1800's, London's River Thames sometimes froze solid. During those centuries, the people of London enjoyed frost fairs on the frozen river. The fairs were carnivals on ice, with stalls selling keepsakes, food, and drinks; athletic matches; skating; and other attractions.

The last frost fair, a five-day event, was held in 1814. The painting shown is of the frost fair held during the winter of 1683-1684.

Earth's warming climate

Evidence of global warming is all around us. **Glaciers** are getting smaller. Ice in the Arctic Ocean is getting thinner. **Deserts** are getting larger. The level of the oceans is rising as the ice that covers land areas melts.

The temperature measurements recorded around the world since 1880 show global warming. They show that **average global temperatures** have been on the rise. From 1900 to 2000, global average temperatures rose by over 1 Fahrenheit degree (0.6 Celsius degree). The year 2014 marked the 38th consecutive year when the global temperature was higher than the long-term average of the 1900's.

Most scientists who study Earth's **atmosphere** believe there is little doubt that today's climate change is due to human activities. They say their **computer models** show that the warming of Earth's **climate** cannot be a natural event.

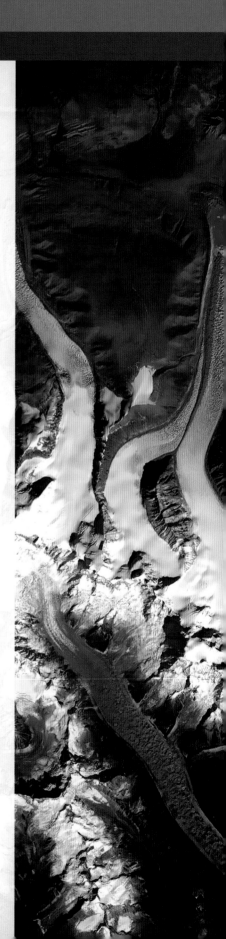

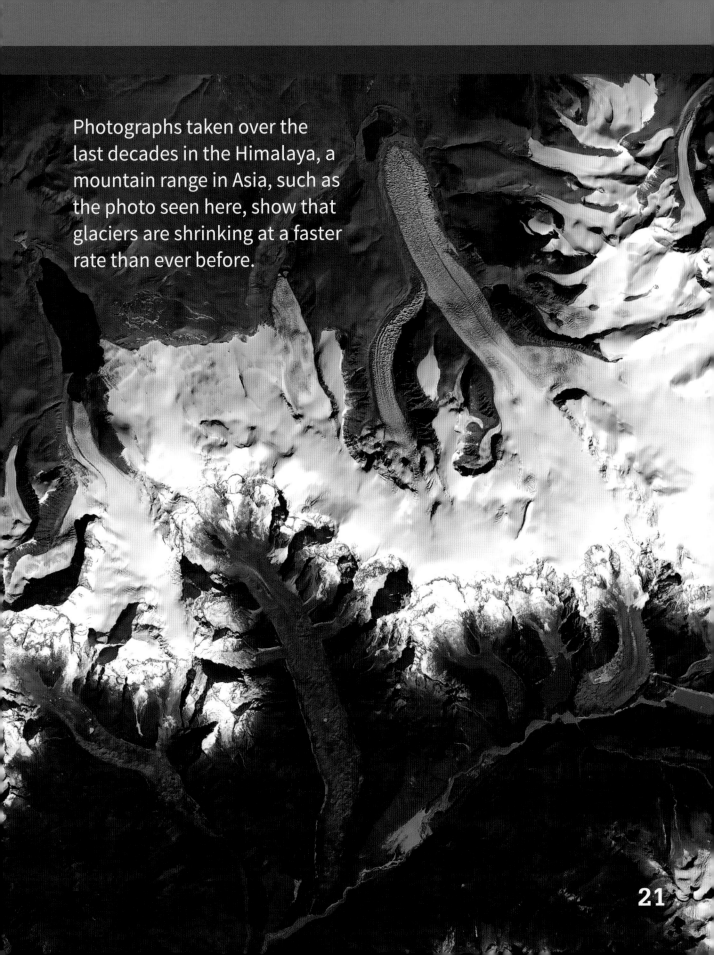

Photographs taken over the last decades in the Himalaya, a mountain range in Asia, such as the photo seen here, show that glaciers are shrinking at a faster rate than ever before.

What is causing global warming?

Global warming, scientists explain, results from the buildup of certain gases in the **atmosphere.** These are gases that slow the escape of heat from Earth's surface. When the planet *absorbs* (takes in) sunlight, it changes sunlight to heat. The gases act like an invisible blanket, holding in the heat. This is called the **greenhouse effect** because it operates like the glass of a greenhouse. The gases are therefore called **greenhouse gases.**

Without the greenhouse effect, Earth would be cold and lifeless. The problem today is that levels of greenhouse gases in the atmosphere are rising so quickly.

The most important greenhouse gas is **carbon dioxide** (CO_2). This gas is produced in large amounts by the burning of **fossil fuels**—coal, oil, and natural gas. They are called fossil fuels because they were formed underground over millions of years. They were produced by the slow decay of fossils— the *remains* (bodies) of ancient plants and animals.

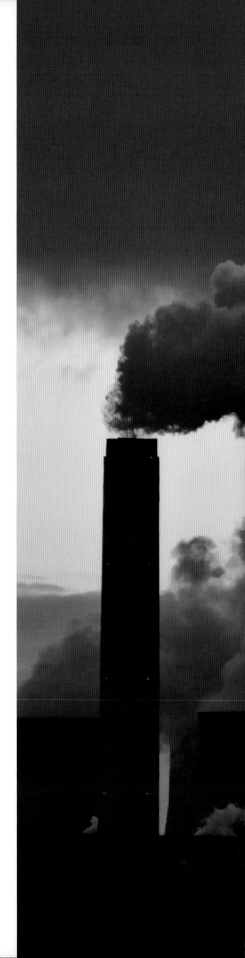

Carbon dioxide, a greenhouse gas, rises out of the tall, narrow smokestack at the far left.

23

Could recent warming be caused naturally?

Some people continue to wonder whether global warming could be caused naturally. But most scientists who study Earth's **atmosphere** say that this cannot be true. They point, in part, to the information from **computer models.**

The researchers also point out that natural climate change takes a long time. In the current ice age, the last glacial cycle gave way to a warming trend about 12,800 years ago. But the current *interglacial* (warming) cycle did not really begin until about 11,500 years ago. That is a span of 1,300 years.

Today's warming is happening in a much shorter time: decades rather than centuries. And it has happened at the same time as a huge amount of **carbon dioxide** (CO_2) was released into the atmosphere. Humans began pouring CO_2 into the air during the Industrial Revolution of the 1800's. With the coming of automobiles in the 1900's, CO_2 in the atmosphere increased even more. Humans now add more than 30 billion tons (27 million metric tons) of CO_2 to the atmosphere every year.

In the early 1800's, the CO_2 content of the atmosphere was about 280 parts per million (ppm). That means that for every 1 million molecules of atmosphere, 280 were CO_2. By 2014, the CO_2 level of the atmosphere had risen to 400 ppm.

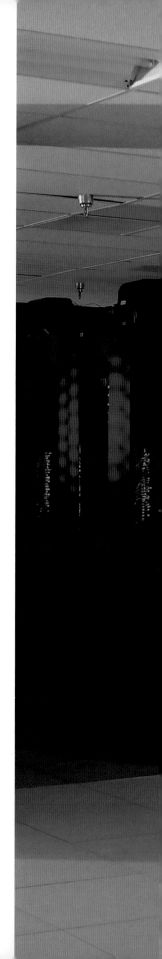

The "Discover" supercomputer at the United States National Aeronautics and Space Administration (NASA) Center for Climate Simulation in Maryland. The supercomputer can run climate *simulations* (electronic models of real-world systems).

The effects of climate change

Scientists have used **computer models** to make likely guesses about, or predict, the future. Their models predict what will happen if global warming continues at its current speed.

One prediction is that ocean levels will rise. The oceans have already risen as much as 8 inches (20 centimeters) since 1900. But the levels are now rising at a faster rate. Since the mid-1990's, sea levels have been increasing by about 0.13 inch (3.2 millimeters) a year. That is approximately twice the rate of the previous 80 years. Rising seas may eventually flood coasts—lands near to oceans—around the world.

Melting ice has been responsible for about half of the sea-level rise. The other half has resulted from a process called *thermal expansion.* That is the *expansion* (increase in size) of water as it becomes warmer. The water of the ocean has gotten warmer by *absorbing* (taking in) heat from the air. About 80 percent of the additional heat in the **atmosphere** has been absorbed by the oceans.

Other outcomes from a warming climate may include the spread of **deserts.** An increase in **tropical** diseases may also be coming. On the other hand, there may be some positive results of global warming. It could, for example, benefit farmers in some regions.

This part of the book will look at these possibilities more closely.

When ocean temperatures get too warm, coral bleaching can happen. That means the coral pushes out the simple, plantlike algae (AL jee) that lives in and feeds it. The coral turns white and may starve.

Melting glaciers and icecaps

One effect of global warming that is easy to see is the melting of mountain **glaciers.** In many parts of the world, glaciers have gotten much smaller.

Other ice is melting, too. Greenland is an island that partly lies in the Arctic Ocean. It is a self-governing territory of the nation of Denmark, in northern Europe. Greenland is almost completely covered by a huge ice sheet. That thick ice has been melting faster and faster. Ice has also been melting from the Antarctic (the land surrounding the South Pole) icecap. If those two enormous bodies of ice were to melt completely, the oceans would rise by an estimated 220 feet (67 meters).

The melting of the Greenland ice sheet could change the climate of northern Europe. It could actually make Europe colder. Winters in northern Europe are kept fairly mild by the Gulf Stream, a warm current of water flowing in the Atlantic Ocean. Air blowing over the Atlantic toward Europe is warmed by the Gulf Stream. But huge amounts of cold water from Greenland could weaken the current.

Far to the north, the U.S. state of Alaska lies on the western edge of the nation of Canada. Two photos taken from the same spot in Alaska show the change in some glaciers. The top photo was taken in 1961, the bottom photo in 2003. The lake has expanded while the ice retreats.

How do we know?

How do we know what glaciers looked like in the past? It's very simple: From photographs. People have been taking pictures of glaciers for more than 100 years. Old photos often show that a glacier was much larger than it is today.

The spread of tropical diseases

Climate change may cause tropical (of the **tropics**) diseases to enter new areas. As places become warmer, disease-carrying insects and **parasites** find new breeding places.

One tropical disease that may spread is **malaria** (muh LAIR ee uh). This illness is caused by a parasite carried by mosquitoes. It strikes at least 220 million people in the tropics every year. About 600,000 of those people die. Malaria happens mostly in hot, low-lying areas. But the disease may start moving into other areas as they grow warmer.

A tropical illness called Chagas (CHAH guhs) disease has moved into the South and Southwest of the United States. This illness is common in Central and South America. It is caused by a parasite carried by a biting insect. Chagas disease can cause heart failure and other serious effects.

Not all diseases that health experts are watching are tropical. Even Arctic regions are seeing an increase in illnesses caused by climate change. One emerging parasite, for example, is sickening musk oxen. Musk oxen are large wild oxen, cattle-like animals, that live on the cold arctic (far northern) plains.

Mosquitoes carry many diseases, including malaria.

The positive effects of climate change

There are likely to be some positive effects from climate change. Many people like to point to the good side of the issue. For example, global warming may open new areas for humans to live in. Houses could become more valuable in some areas.

There are also possible benefits for farmers. Global warming is likely to lengthen growing seasons in crop-growing regions. It will also allow farming in some areas that are now too cold for farming. Siberia is an area within Russia, in far northern Asia. It is a huge area with few people. Climate change could possibly turn this freezing land into farmland.

Agriculture may also benefit from the **carbon dioxide** (CO_2) that is being added to the **atmosphere.** Green plants use CO_2 and the energy of sunlight to grow. With more CO_2, many crops—as well as trees, grasses, and other plants—will grow more.

Unfortunately, the pluses are likely to be outweighed by minuses. Weeds will flourish along with crops. Some present-day farmlands will be lost to **drought** and the expansion of **deserts.** Many low-lying areas will be under water once oceans rise. Great movements of people could occur as both croplands and homelands disappear.

Extreme weather in a warming world

Weather events require energy. That energy—in the form of heat—comes from the sun. Because of global warming, more heat is available. Earth's increased **greenhouse effect** holds the heat in the **atmosphere** and the oceans. Global warming is likely to fuel an increase in *extreme* (strong and violent) weather.

Some strong winter storms have already been tied to **climate** change. But other kinds of extreme weather may also be on the rise. Those dramatic weather events include **hurricanes, tornadoes,** and heat waves.

The world has always experienced terrible storms, hurricanes, and heat waves. The question is whether that kind of extreme weather has gotten worse and more usual. More important, what does the future hold? Will climate change cause extreme weather events to become increasingly violent and common?

A number of things add to the likelihood of a place experiencing extreme weather. But the connection between weather and its causes is complicated. This makes it impossible to blame any particular disaster on climate change. However, **computer models** suggest that global warming could make storms more dangerous or more frequent overall.

Hurricanes and tornadoes

Hurricanes and **tornadoes** are Earth's most violent weather events. They are both rotating storms, but they differ greatly in many ways.

Hurricanes form over warm water near the equator. A large cloud system begins to *rotate* (turn), *absorbing* (taking in) heat from the water. As the rotation speeds up, the system is called a **tropical** storm. When wind speeds reach 74 miles (119 kilometers) per hour, the storm is officially a hurricane. In Asia, hurricanes are called *typhoons* or *tropical cyclones.* These storms are incredibly powerful. Wind speeds may be more than 150 miles (240 kilometers) an hour. The storms also produce heavy rains. And they push a mass of water called a **storm surge** from the ocean onto the land.

A tornado is a rapidly spinning, funnel-shaped cloud. Tornadoes develop in huge thunderstorms called *supercells.* Within the storm, a large column of air begins to rotate *horizontally* (level to the ground). Rising air in the supercell tilts the rotating air column from horizontal to *vertical* (up and down). If the rotating column descends from the cloud, it is a tornado.

A tornado can be up to 1 mile (1.6 kilometers) wide and have wind speeds of as much as 300 miles (480 kilometers) per hour. As it moves along the ground, a tornado can cause terrible damage.

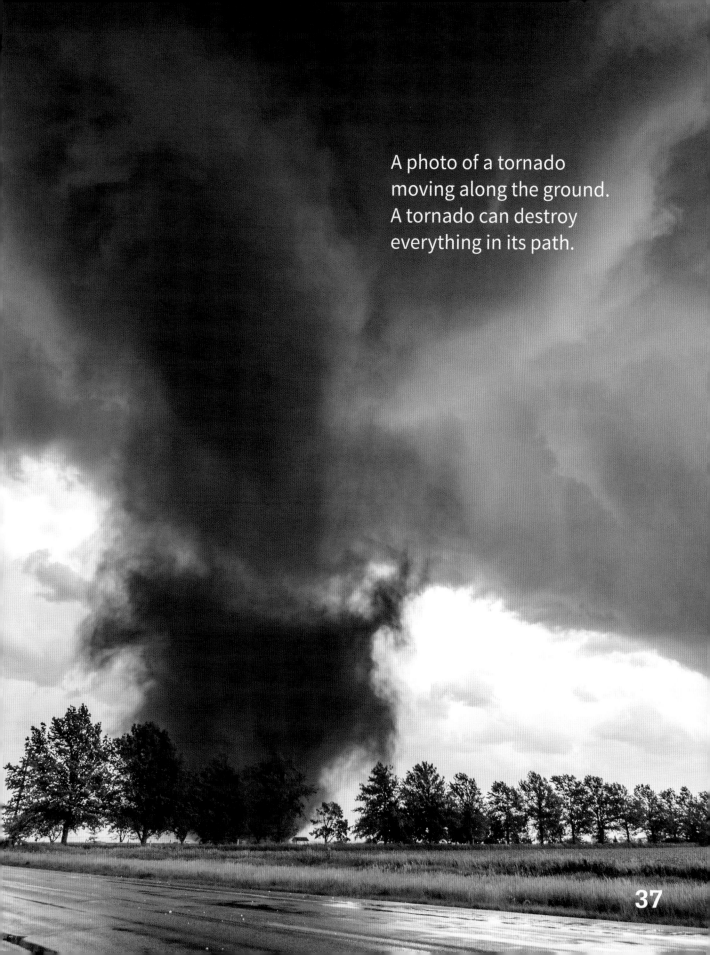

A photo of a tornado moving along the ground. A tornado can destroy everything in its path.

Hurricane Katrina

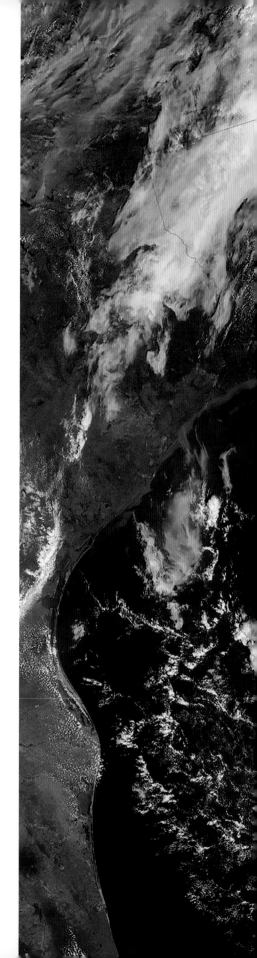

One of the most destructive **hurricanes** in United States history occurred on August 29, 2005. On that day, Hurricane Katrina struck the coast of the Gulf of Mexico in the United States. The storm caused death and damage all along the coast. But it was the city of New Orleans, Louisiana, that suffered most.

After developing in the Caribbean Sea, the hurricane crossed Florida. It then moved into the Gulf of Mexico, gaining strength. For a time it had wind speeds of about 175 miles (280 kilometers) per hour. Katrina weakened before hitting the coast, but it was still a powerful storm.

In New Orleans, the worst damage occurred when levees failed. Levees are barriers made of dirt built to keep out water and protect an area from floods. Because much of New Orleans lies below sea level, flooding is always a danger. Breaks in the levees allowed the water of a nearby lake to fill the city.

The hurricane caused more than 1,800 deaths, mostly in Louisiana. It caused an estimated US $108 billion in property damage. That figure made Katrina the costliest hurricane ever in dollar terms.

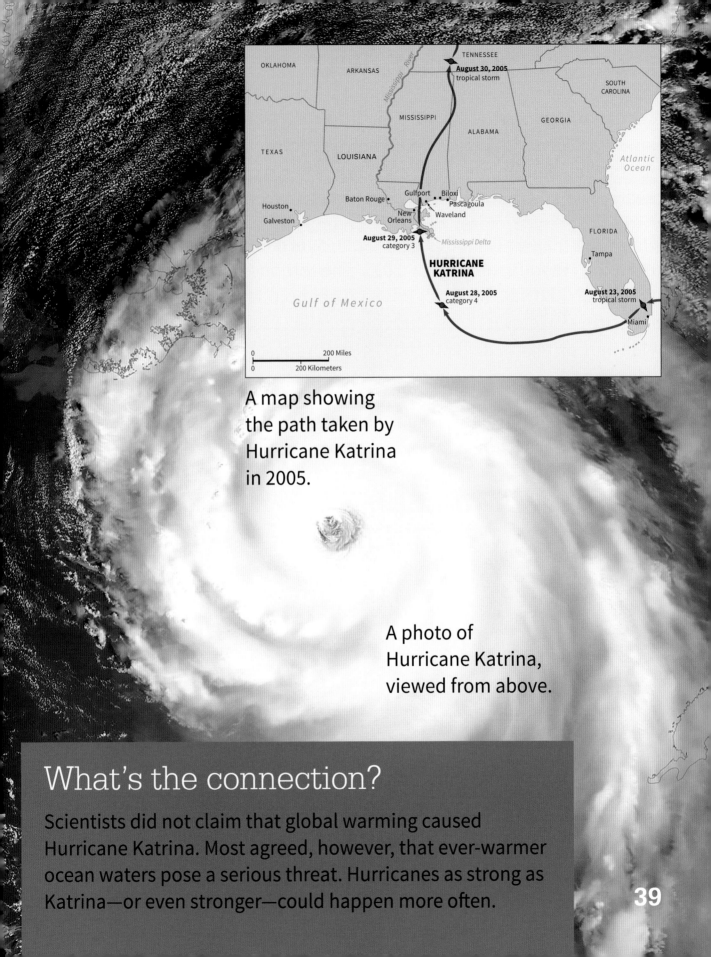

OKLAHOMA
ARKANSAS
TENNESSEE
August 30, 2005
tropical storm
Mississippi River
SOUTH
CAROLINA
MISSISSIPPI
GEORGIA
ALABAMA
TEXAS
LOUISIANA
Atlantic
Ocean
Gulfport
Biloxi
Pascagoula
Baton Rouge
Waveland
Houston
New
Orleans
FLORIDA
Galveston
Mississippi Delta
August 29, 2005
category 3
Tampa
**HURRICANE
KATRINA**
Gulf of Mexico
August 28, 2005
category 4
August 23, 2005
tropical storm
Miami

0   200 Miles
0   200 Kilometers

A map showing
the path taken by
Hurricane Katrina
in 2005.

A photo of
Hurricane Katrina,
viewed from above.

What's the connection?

Scientists did not claim that global warming caused
Hurricane Katrina. Most agreed, however, that ever-warmer
ocean waters pose a serious threat. Hurricanes as strong as
Katrina—or even stronger—could happen more often.

39

The Joplin tornado

Most **tornadoes** in the United States occur in a central region known as **Tornado Alley.** There, moist air from the south meets cool air from the north and west. These collisions create the huge thunderstorms that produce tornadoes.

One of the biggest tornadoes ever seen smashed into the city of Joplin, Missouri, on May 22, 2011. The tornado had winds faster than 200 miles (320 kilometers) per hour. It left a path of destruction about three-fourths of a mile (1.2 kilometers) wide and six miles (10 kilometers) long. Property damage was estimated at US $3 billion.

At least 161 people died in the disaster and more than 1,000 were injured. The Joplin tornado ranks as the deadliest U.S. twister since 1947.

A map of the U.S. shows the number of tornadoes that happen, on average, each year in 10,000 square miles (25,900 square kilometers) of area. The darkest area at the center is Tornado Alley, which stretches across the Midwestern and Southern states, especially Texas, Oklahoma, Kansas, Nebraska, and Iowa.

None to 2	6 to 8
2 to 4	8 to 10
4 to 6	More than 10

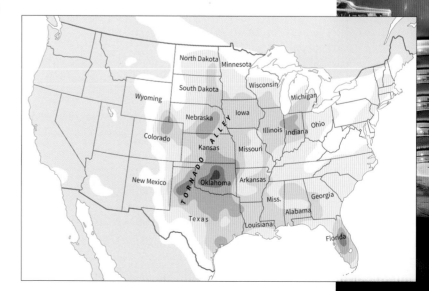

U.S. President Barack Obama greets Joplin residents after a 2011 tornado.

Heat waves

In the summer of 2003, the continent of Europe experienced a terrible heat wave. Health experts said about 80,000 people died from the heat.

That heat wave was just the beginning. Around the world, hotter summers have become usual. Europe suffered from horrible heat again in 2013. Four nations elsewhere—Australia, China, Japan, and Korea—also baked in severe heat. Australia's heat wave was the worst in its history. On one day, the temperature in Sydney was 114.4 °F (45.8 °C). As a coastal city, Sydney's normal high temperature had been about 86 °F (30 °C).

Scientists believe that the 2013 heat waves were caused mostly by global warming. They predict more summers with punishing heat—including in the United States.

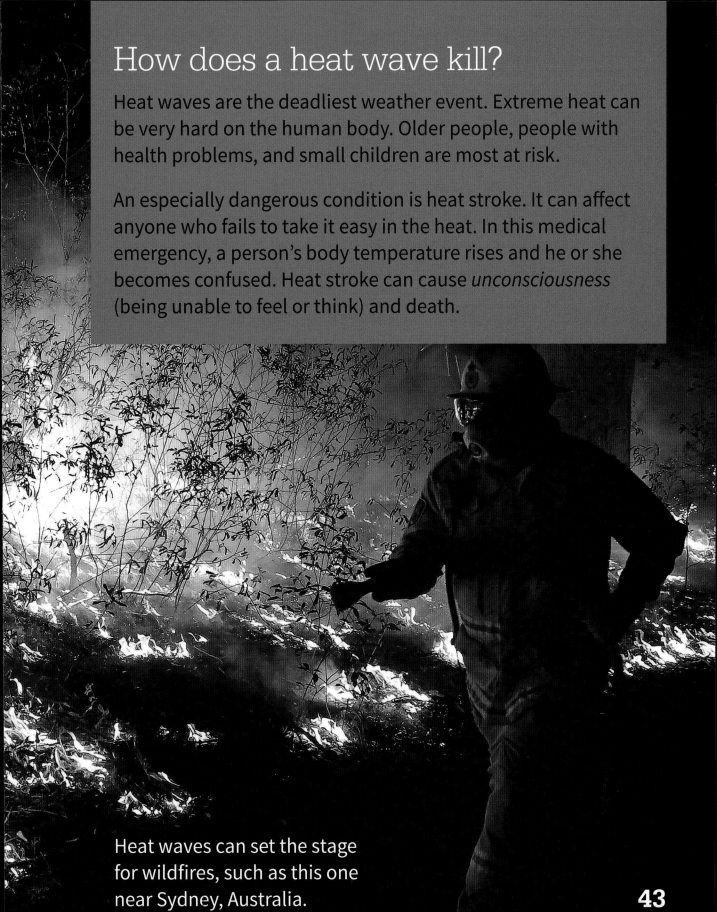

How does a heat wave kill?

Heat waves are the deadliest weather event. Extreme heat can be very hard on the human body. Older people, people with health problems, and small children are most at risk.

An especially dangerous condition is heat stroke. It can affect anyone who fails to take it easy in the heat. In this medical emergency, a person's body temperature rises and he or she becomes confused. Heat stroke can cause *unconsciousness* (being unable to feel or think) and death.

Heat waves can set the stage
for wildfires, such as this one
near Sydney, Australia.

43

What can we do?

Scientists say we must act to control global warming. To do that, we need to reduce the production of greenhouse gases. That will likely require us to reduce our use of **fossil fuels.**

Cars and trucks burn large amounts of gasoline. A move to electric cars would greatly reduce gasoline use.

Most electricity is generated by burning fossil fuels. For the time being, that will not change. But there is a way to stop the release of **carbon dioxide** (CO_2) from power plants. It is called carbon sequestration (SEE kwehs TRAY shuhn). This technology involves capturing the CO_2 produced by burning fuel and storing it underground.

Developing renewable *energy* (energy that can be used over and over) may also decrease our use of **fossil fuels.** Solar energy and wind power are today's leading sources of renewable energy.

Young people can help combat global warming. They can encourage their parents to drive less and to use energy-efficient appliances and light bulbs.

Energy farms use wind and sunlight—natural sources of power—to create electricity. Such energy does not release large amounts of carbon dioxide into the **atmosphere.**

GLOSSARY and RESOURCES

atmosphere The mass of gases that surrounds a planet.

average temperature A temperature for a given time period. For example, in a month, the temperature for each day is totaled, and that number is divided by the number of days in the month, to get the average temperature.

carbon dioxide A colorless, *odorless* (with no smell) gas found in the atmospheres of many planets, including Earth. On Earth, green plants must get carbon dioxide from the atmosphere to live and grow. Animals breathe out the gas when their bodies convert food into energy and living tissue. Carbon dioxide is also created by the burning of any substance that contains carbon, such as coal and gasoline.

climate The weather of a place averaged over a length of time.

computer model Sets of mathematical equations that represent things or ideas.

desert A barren region of Earth's surface that receives little rainfall.

drought When the average rainfall for an area drops far below the normal amount for a long time.

fossil fuel An energy-providing material—coal, oil, or natural gas—formed from the long-dead remains of living things.

glacier A large mass of ice that flows slowly because of gravity.

greenhouse effect A warming of the lower atmosphere and surface of a planet by a process involving sunlight, gases, and atmospheric particles. On Earth, the greenhouse effect began long before humans existed. However, the amounts of heat-trapping atmospheric gases, called greenhouse gases, have increased since the mid-1800's, when modern industry became widespread.

hurricane A powerful, swirling storm that begins over a warm sea.

lake-effect snow Snowstorms caused by cold air passing over large bodies of warmer water.

malaria One of the most widespread and threatening parasitic diseases that affect human beings. Malaria is caused by infection with parasites passed by female mosquitoes.

parasite A living thing that feeds off another living thing, called a host.

plate tectonics Earth has an outer shell made up of about 30 rigid pieces called tectonic plates. The plates move on a layer of rock that is so hot it flows, even though it remains solid. The plates are moving very slowly at speeds up to about 4 inches (10 centimeters) per year. They have been moving about for hundreds of millions of years.

pollen Tiny grains that are produced in the male organs of flowering and cone-bearing plants. Seeds develop after pollen is transferred from the male part of a plant to the female part.

storm surge A sudden rush of waves onto land caused by strong winds.

tornado A tornado is a rapidly *rotating* (turning) column of air (known as a vortex) that has reached the ground.

Tornado Alley A region in the central U.S. that has more tornadoes on average than anywhere else in the world. Tornado Alley includes parts of the states of Texas, Oklahoma, Kansas, and Nebraska.

tropics Regions of Earth that lie within about 1,600 miles (2,570 kilometers) north and south of the equator. Most places in the tropics have warm to hot temperatures the year around.

Books:

Kiesbye, Stefan. *Are Natural Disasters Increasing?* Detroit: Greenhaven, 2010.

Green, Dan, and Simon Basher. *Climate Change.* New York: Kingfisher, 2014.

Kostigen, Thomas. *Extreme Weather: Surviving Tornadoes, Sandstorms, Hailstorms, Blizzards, Hurricanes, and More!* Washington, D.C.: National Geographic, 2014.

Rothschild, David de. *Earth Matters.* New York: DK Pub., 2011.

Websites:

NASA – Climate Change and Global Warming
http://climate.nasa.gov/

National Geographic – Global Warming
http://environment.nationalgeographic.com/environment/global-warming/

United States Environmental Protection Agency – A Student's Guide to Global Climate Change
http://www.epa.gov/climatestudents/

United States Environmental Protection Agency – Weather and Climate
http://www.epa.gov/climate/climatechange/science/indicators/weather-climate/

Think about it

Why do warmer temperatures lead to illnesses infecting people in areas in which they had not previously been a problem?

[Most living things have a range—an area in which temperature and other things help them to survive. Many of the illnesses that are becoming more common in new areas are spread by mosquitoes or other insects. Those warm-temperature insects are able to survive in new areas as those areas become warmer. And, they bring such diseases as Chagas disease and malaria with them as they move in.]

47

INDEX